Dd

drive

Ee

Ff

My Giant
PICTURE DICTIONARY

frog

Jj

Illustrated by Robert C. Durham

jacket

logs

Pp

pair

DERRYDALE BOOKS
New York

raccoon

Vv

van

yawn

Ww

well

x-ray

Zz

zero

$$-\frac{2}{0}$$

Aa

address

An **address** is the number, street, city, state, and zip code of where you live. John wrote his grandmother's **address** on the envelope before he mailed the letter.

acrobat

An **acrobat** is a person who learns to perform difficult exercises or stunts. The daring circus **acrobat** swings on a trapeze high above the crowd.

adjective

An **adjective** is a word that describes a person, place, or thing. Words like *happy, big,* and *soft* are **adjectives**. Ann used the **adjectives** *shiny* and *red* to describe her new bicycle.

across

Across means to go from one side to the other. Sandy jumped **across** the puddle without getting her feet wet.

adult

An **adult** is a person who is grown up. Your parents and teachers are **adults**. Be sure there is an **adult** with you when you cross the street.

act

To **act** means to pretend to be someone or something else. My brother likes to ride his toy horse and **act** like a cowboy.

after

After means later in time. You should brush your teeth **after** eating meals or sweets. **After** also means behind. The children went down the slide one **after** another.

again

To do something **again** means to do it one more time. If you like a special story, you may ask to hear it **again**.

agree

When people **agree** with each other, they have the same ideas or feelings and want the same things. After the game, the players shook hands and **agreed** that both teams had played well.

alive

If something is **alive**, it is able to grow. Plants, animals, and people are **alive**. To keep flowers **alive**, you must be sure that they get sun and water.

alphabet

The **alphabet** is the set of all the letters that make up the words of a language. Our **alphabet**, A to Z, has 26 letters. Can you name all the letters in the **alphabet**?

ambulance

An **ambulance** is a special car that carries people who are sick or hurt. An **ambulance** must sometimes drive very fast to a hospital.

animals

Animals are all living things that are not plants. An ant, a worm, a whale, a robin, a cat, and a tiger are all **animals**. You see many different **animals** at a pet shop.

answer

When you **answer** someone you say or write something back. You also **answer** the telephone or the doorbell. When the telephone rang, John **answered** it.

any

Any means one or some. Paul had cereal for breakfast because there weren't **any** eggs left.

5

aquarium

An **aquarium** is a glass tank filled with water. Many kinds of fish can live in a **aquarium**. The pet shop keeps angelfish in one of its **aquariums**.

arrow

An **arrow** is a mark that points in one direction. A huge red **arrow** showed the cars which direction to go.

artist

An **artist** is a person who draws or paints. **Artists** may use paint, pen, pencil, or chalk to make pictures. The **artist** painted a picture of a little boy and his dog.

ask

When you want to know something, you **ask** a question. You might **ask** *who, what, why, when,* or *where.* If you can't solve the problem, **ask** the teacher to help you.

attach

To **attach** one thing to another means to put them together tightly. Fred used tape to **attach** the note to the door.

author

An **author** is a person who writes books or stories. The **author** uses a typewriter to write his stories. Who is your favorite **author**?

autumn

Autumn is the name of the season that comes after summer. **Autumn** is another name for fall. In the **autumn** the weather gets cooler, the leaves turn colors, and school starts again!

awning

An **awning** is a small roof that sticks out over a window to keep off the rain or sun. The **awning** over the restaurant window kept the hot sun off the people inside.

Bb

balance

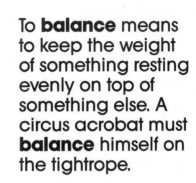

To **balance** means to keep the weight of something resting evenly on top of something else. A circus acrobat must **balance** himself on the tightrope.

backpack

A **backpack** is a special bag that you wear on your back to carry books or camping supplies. Sam carried a **backpack** and a sleeping bag on the long hike.

ballet

Ballet is a beautiful, graceful kind of dancing performed on a stage. Dancers in costumes do special steps, turns, and leaps. The dancer started studying **ballet** when she was a small child.

badminton

Badminton is an outdoor game. Players use rackets to hit a piece called a *birdie* back and forth over a net. In the summer, the children play **badminton** in the backyard.

balloon

A **balloon** is a brightly colored rubber bag that can be filled with air or helium. You often see **balloons** at birthday parties, parades, or other celebrations.

bake

When you **bake**, you cook food in an oven. You can **bake** meat or bread or sweets like cookies and cakes. They **bake** delicious cake at the bakery on Main Street.

bank

A **bank** is a safe place to keep money. Mother went to the **bank** to take out some money. Sally keeps her money in a small **bank** on her desk.

barbell

A **barbell** is a piece of equipment used for exercising. Weights are attached to both ends of a metal bar. The weight lifter held the heavy **barbell** above his head for a few seconds.

bear

A **bear** is a large, furry animal that lives in the woods. **Bears** can be white, black, or brown. A trained **bear** rode a unicycle at the circus.

barn

A **barn** is a large building on a farm where animals are kept. Feed or farm machinery also may be stored there. The loft in the red **barn** was filled with hay.

beautiful

When you see something that is very pretty and pleasing you say it is **beautiful**. Kim thought that the new pink dress her mother bought her was **beautiful**.

barrel

A **barrel** is a tall, round container usually made of wood. At an old-fashioned general store, you can buy pickles out of a **barrel**.

beaver

A **beaver** is a small, furry animal with sharp teeth and a wide, flat tail. A **beaver** builds a home of mud and sticks, which makes a dam across a stream.

battery

A **battery** produces electrical power to make things, like cars, run. The mechanic at the service station said the car wouldn't start because it needed a new **battery**.

before

Before means earlier in time. Mother gave the baby a bath **before** she put him to bed. **Before** also means in front of. Donna sang **before** a huge audience.

beg

To **beg** means to ask for something that you want very badly. One of my dog's tricks is to sit up and **beg** for a dog biscuit.

bend

If you **bend** something, you change it from being straight to being curved. The mechanic had to **bend** over and reach under the hood of the car to check the oil.

believe

To **believe** means to think that a person is being honest or that an idea is true. If you make a wish on a star, do you **believe** it will come true?

bicycle

A **bicycle** is a vehicle that people ride. It has two wheels, handlebars, a seat, and pedals that you push to make it move. Mark rides his **bicycle** to school every day.

belong

To **belong** means to be owned by someone. This lunch box **belongs** to Alexandra. It has her name on it. **Belong** also means to be where it should be. Milk **belongs** in the refrigerator.

billboard

A **billboard** is a large outdoor sign that displays advertisements or special messages. A **billboard** next to the road tells about fresh fruit sold at the farm ahead.

bench

A **bench** is a long seat for two or more people. After Grandma and Grandpa take a walk in the park, they like to sit on the **bench** and feed the pigeons.

binoculars

Binoculars are instruments that make faraway objects seem larger and closer. Bird-watchers use **binoculars** to get a better look at birds in trees or flying overhead.

bird

A **bird** is an animal that has wings and feathers. An owl, an eagle, a penguin, a duck, and a turkey are all **birds**. A chickadee ate the seeds Jill put in the **bird** feeder.

book

A **book** is a set of pages that contains words or pictures. Some **books** tell about real people and places. Some **books** tell imaginary stories. Libraries have many different **books** people can borrow.

birthday

Your **birthday** is the day you were born. You celebrate being one year older on your **birthday** each year. Janet invited all her friends to her **birthday** party.

boots

Boots are shoes that cover your feet and legs to protect them from rain, snow, or mud. **Boots** can be made of rubber or leather. The campers wore strong leather hiking **boots** to climb the mountain.

bloom

To **bloom** means to produce flowers. Roses, irises, daisies, and marigolds **bloom** in a summer garden.

bricks

Bricks are small, red clay blocks used in building walls, chimneys, and houses. Workers laid the **bricks** in straight, neat rows.

boat

A **boat** is a vehicle that travels in the water carrying people or things. The wind makes a sailboat go, oars make a rowboat go, and engines make motorboats go.

briefcase

A **briefcase** is a container for carrying books or papers. Tim's mother brings her work home in a **briefcase**.

broom

A **broom** is a kind of brush. It has a long handle and is used to sweep up dirt and trash. Uncle Bob used a **broom** to clean off the front porch.

build

When you **build**, you put materials together to make something. Wood and nails are often used to **build** houses.

bulldozer

A **bulldozer** is a machine used to clear land and make roads. On the front of the **bulldozer** is a huge blade that pushes dirt, rocks, or trees.

bulletin board

A **bulletin board** hangs on the wall and is used to display important announcements or papers. Ms. Collins put the best stories on the **bulletin board**.

bus

A **bus** is a large vehicle with many seats that carries people from place to place. There are school **buses**, city **buses**, and **buses** that travel on highways to take people long distances.

busy

When you are **busy**, you have many things to do. Emily was **busy** making cookies for the school picnic.

butterfly

A **butterfly** is an insect with large, brightly colored wings. In the meadow in the spring, there seems to be a **butterfly** on every flower.

buy

To **buy** something, means you pay money so that it can belong to you. Danny went to the fruit stand to **buy** an apple for lunch.

ANIMALS

Animals live all over the world. Some live in jungles or forests, while others live in the mountains or near the water.

The **lion**, **cheetah**, and **leopard** belong to the cat family. They live on the plains of Africa where they hunt for food.

Zebras, **gazelles**, and **antelopes** also live in Africa. They travel in herds, grazing on the plentiful grass of the plains. The **rhinoceros** stays close to the watering hole, while the **giraffe** prefers the leaves of bushes and trees at the edge of the plain.

The **okapi** lives in the rain forest, where its special markings help it blend into the surroundings, while the **hippopotamus** can usually be found near a muddy swamp.

The **gorilla**, **baboon**, **mandrill**, and **orangutan** are all members of the ape family. They carry their babies on their backs and live in forests and jungles, where there are plenty of leaves and fruit to eat.

Some unusual animals come from South America, including the **llama**, a relative of the **camel**; the **iguana**, a prehistoric-looking lizard; the **anteater**, whose long nose helps it find insects to eat; the **armadillo**, whose hard shell looks like a suit of armor; and the **sloth**, who spends its days hanging in tree branches.

Australia is home to such animals as the **kangaroo**, who carries its babies in a pouch, and the **koala bear**, who eats only the leaves of the eucalyptus tree.

The **walrus**, with its many layers of fat, and the **polar bear** with its thick white coat of fur, are both well suited to the ice and snow of **their** home in the arctic.

leopard

lion

ocelot

cheetah

coyote

hyena

lynx

gorilla

sloth

mandrill

baboon

orangutan

anteater

camel

giraffe

llama

zebra

okapi

gnu

gazelle

antelope

armadillo

bala bear

ring-tailed lemur

buffalo

yak

kangaroo

bison

black bear

walrus

polar bear

hippopotamus

panda

crocodile

aardvark

alligator

rhinoceros

iguana

cobra

boa constrictor

call

When you **call** someone, you speak with a loud voice. Mother **called** the children inside for lunch. You may also use a telephone to **call** someone.

cage

A **cage** is a kind of container for animals to live in or to be carried in. In a **cage** at the pet store is a parrot that says "hello."

camera

A **camera** is a machine that uses light and mirrors to make a picture. It's fun to use a **camera** to take photos of your family and friends and the places you like to go.

cake

A **cake** is a sweet food that is baked. It is made from batter that usually contains flour, sugar, butter, and eggs. Paul's sister baked him a chocolate **cake** for his birthday.

candle

A **candle** is a piece of wax with a string in the middle. When the string is lit, the **candle** burns to give off light. Many, many years ago, a **candle** was the only kind of light in people's homes.

calendar

A **calendar** is a chart of all the days of the year. James put a big red circle around his birthday on the **calendar**.

car

A **car** is a four-wheeled vehicle in which people ride that is powered by an engine. The family traveled by **car** to visit their friends in the next town.

careful

When you are **careful**, you do something slowly, paying attention to everything. Susan was **careful** not to spill any juice when she poured it into the glass.

carry

When you **carry** something, you move from place to place while holding it. Laura was surprised to see the waiter **carry** the heavy tray above his head.

cash register

A **cash register** is a machine in a store that tells the cost of every item sold. The **cash register** has a drawer for keeping money and making change.

cement mixer

A **cement mixer** is a machine that makes the cement needed for buildings and roads. At the construction site for the new bank, the **cement mixer** turns all day long.

chandelier

A **chandelier** is a fancy light that hangs from a ceiling. The dining room **chandelier** was draped with colorful streamers for the party.

change

To **change** something means to make it different from the way it was. You can **change** your clothes, your plans, or your mind. The children **change** into sneakers when they go outside.

chest

A **chest** is a piece of furniture used for storing things. A **chest** often looks like a large wooden box. Great-Aunt May kept her wedding dress in an old oak **chest**.

children

Children are young people. Boys and girls are **children**. How many **children** are there in your family?

choose

When you **choose**, you decide to pick one thing instead of another. Jessie's brother always **chooses** strawberry ice cream, but she always **chooses** chocolate.

clown

A **clown** is someone who makes people laugh. The circus **clown** wore baggy pants and had a big red nose.

circle

A **circle** is a shape that is perfectly round. A wheel, a plate, and a ball are all **circles**.

collection

A **collection** is a group of objects put together to be shown or studied. You may collect stamps, coins, or stickers. At the science museum, there is a beautiful **collection** of butterflies.

city

A **city** is a large place with a lot of buildings and streets, where many people live and work. Terry likes the excitement of life in the **city**, but his cousins like the quiet of the country.

computer

A **computer** is a machine that gathers information and solves problems very quickly. The children practiced spelling and math on the **computer**.

climb

To **climb** means to move up something, often by using hands and feet. Henry **climbed** the ladder to the top of the slide.

control tower

A **control tower** is the place at the airport from which planes are told when to land and when to take off. The pilot called the **control tower** to see if the runway was clear for her to land.

copy

To **copy** means to make something exactly like something else. This log cabin is a **copy** of one used long ago by a pioneer family.

corner

A **corner** is a place at which two sides or edges meet. It is also the place where two roads cross each other. There was a small mouse sitting in the **corner** of the room.

correct

Correct means the right one. The teacher gave the boy a blue ribbon because he gave the **correct** answer on the test. To **correct** means to make something right. **Correct** the words you spelled wrong.

count

When you **count**, you name the numbers in order. **Count** from 1 to 10. When you **count** something, you tell how many there are. The teacher asked me to **count** the new pencils.

cow

A **cow** is an animal that lives on a farm and gives milk. The big, brown **cow** wears a bell so the farmer knows where to find her.

crane

A **crane** is a machine used in building to raise and lower heavy objects. The workman attached the pipe to the cable, and the **crane** lifted it.

curious

If you are **curious** about something, you want to know about it. The kitten was **curious** about what was in the big box.

curtains

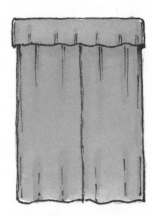

Curtains are cloth coverings for windows. **Curtains** are used to add color or to give you privacy. Mother made new **curtains** for the living room.

Dd

daydream

A **daydream** is a pleasant, imaginary thought about something you wish might happen. In a **daydream**, Adam pictured himself as an astronaut.

dance

When you **dance**, you move in time to the beat of music. Jane likes to **dance**, so she is going to take ballet lessons.

decide

If you **decide** something, you have thought about it and have made a choice. John **decided** to buy the model plane instead of the train.

dark

When it's **dark**, there is no light and you can't see. Joey kept a flashlight in his room so he could see in the **dark**.

definition

A **definition** is a statement that tells the meaning of a word. You can find the **definition** of many words in a dictionary like this one.

date

The **date** is the day, the month, and the year. You can find today's **date** on the front page of the newspaper.

deliver

To **deliver** means to take something and give it to another person. Mary **delivered** the party invitations herself.

dentist

A **dentist** is a doctor who helps you take care of your teeth. Be sure to brush your teeth every day and visit the **dentist** for regular checkups.

dish

A **dish** is a container to hold the food that you eat. Mother served the salad in a **dish** that her grandmother had given her.

desk

A **desk** is a piece of furniture with a flat top that you can use for writing, drawing, or reading. Warren likes to write letters at the **desk** in his room.

divide

When you **divide** something, you separate it into parts or groups. Mary **divided** the pie into four equal parts.

dinosaur

A **dinosaur** is an enormous animal that lived on Earth millions of years ago. A **dinosaur** looked like a huge lizard, with a long body and tail, and short legs.

doctor

A **doctor** is a person who helps you stay healthy and helps you get well if you are sick. The **doctor** listened to my heart with a stethoscope.

discover

If you **discover** something, you find it or find out about it for the first time. When Danny reeled in his fishing line, he **discovered** that a fish had taken his bait.

dolphin

A **dolphin** is a kind of small whale. A **dolphin** is a gentle, smart animal that can be playful or learn to do tricks.

drafting table

A **drafting table** is a piece of furniture that has a flat top that can be tilted up. A **drafting table** is used by artists, architects, or workers who make detailed drawings.

dragonfly

A **dragonfly** is an insect with a long body and large wings. A **dragonfly** rested on the picnic table in the summer sun.

dresser

A **dresser** is a piece of furniture with drawers. Nicky was in such a hurry that he left the **dresser** drawer open when he took out his sweater.

drip

To **drip** means to fall in drops. A leaky faucet might **drip** water. On a hot day, ice cream in a cone might **drip** on your clothes.

drive

When you **drive** something, you control how and where it moves. Every child in the store wanted to **drive** the new toy car.

drop

If you **drop** something, you let it fall. Rachel tried to carry too much at once and **dropped** her books.

drum

A **drum** is a musical instrument that can be beaten with your hands or with a special stick. Joey tapped out the song on his new **drum**.

duck

A **duck** is a swimming bird with webbed feet. The **duck** paddled out onto the lake.

Ee

edge

The **edge** of something is the point where it begins or ends. Margaret left the flower pot on the **edge** of the shelf.

early

Early means near the beginning or before something is due. The rooster wakes up **early** in the morning, just as the sun comes up.

either

Either means one or the other. You may wear **either** the red socks or the blue ones, but not both.

earth

Earth is the layer of soil covering the ground. The farmer turns over the dark, rich **earth** before planting the garden. **Earth** is the planet we live on. The **Earth** is round.

elephant

An **elephant** is a huge animal with a long trunk and a tough hide. There are many **elephants** in Africa and Asia. In the parade, one **elephant** wore a bright green blanket.

easel

An **easel** is a stand that holds the paper and paints you need for making a picture. Melissa stood at the **easel** and painted a picture that filled the page.

empty

If something is **empty**, it has nothing in it. The lion's cage was **empty** because the lion was performing in the circus ring.

21

encourage

To **encourage** means to give someone help and support when things seem difficult. The cheering crowd **encouraged** the runner to keep going even though he was tired.

escape

To **escape** means to get away from somewhere, usually very quickly. The mouse **escaped** from the cat through a hole in the wall.

end

The **end** of something is its last moment or its farthest place. At the **end** of the day, Jenny puts away her toys and goes to bed. Pat walked to the **end** of the diving board and dove into the water.

every

Every means each person or thing in a group. **Every** light in the house was on last night.

enjoy

If you **enjoy** something, you are pleased with it. Meg and Paul **enjoy** camping out at the lake in the summer.

exercise

When you **exercise**, you use the muscles of your body in order to keep them strong and healthy. Hank's father likes to **exercise** by walking two miles every day.

equal

When things are **equal**, they are the same size, number, or quality. John made three **equal** piles of apples.

explain

To **explain** something is to make it clear by describing it in great detail. The directions **explain** how to put together the model airplane.

Ff

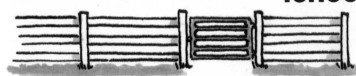
fence

A **fence** is an outdoor wall that is used to keep things in or out. A **fence** may be made of wood, stone, brick, or wire. The white **fence** around the pasture keeps the cows from wandering away.

family

Your **family** is your father, mother, brothers, and sisters. It also includes your grandparents, aunts, uncles, and cousins. My **family** eats dinner together every night.

fireplace

A **fireplace** is an open place in a chimney where a fire can be safely burned. Some people burn wood in a **fireplace** to keep their homes warm.

fan

A **fan** is a machine that makes a breeze to cool you. On hot summer nights, you put a **fan** in the window to blow a cool breeze through the house.

first

When something is **first** it comes before everything else. Mary was the **first** in line to buy a ticket.

fast

Fast means to move or do something very quickly. Rabbits usually move very **fast**, but turtles move very slowly.

fish

A **fish** is an animal that lives in water. Some **fish**, like trout, live in ponds and streams. Other **fish** live in the ocean.

fix

When you **fix** something you make it work again. The boy asked his father to help him **fix** the broken kite.

forget

To **forget** means to be unable to remember. Jim **forgot** his books when he left the park.

flat

If something is **flat**, it is smooth, straight, and even. The girl spread her towel out to dry on the big, **flat** rock.

forklift

A **forklift** is a machine that lifts and carries heavy objects. On the front of the **forklift** are two long metal bars that slide under an object in order to pick it up.

flower

A **flower** is a plant that has pretty, colorful blossoms. I brought Grandmother some **flowers** from our garden.

fossil

A **fossil** is a mark left in rock by animals or plants that lived millions of years ago. There is a large collection of **fossils** at the natural history museum.

follow

Follow means to come after something. The ducklings **followed** their mother across the pond. **Follow** also means to obey instructions. If you **follow** my directions, you'll get there in ten minutes.

fountain

A **fountain** is a spray of water that flows into a small pool. In the park, water flows out of a **fountain** that looks like a fish.

fox

A **fox** is an animal with pointed ears and a long bushy tail that lives in the woods. We saw a small red **fox** disappear into its den at the bottom of a tree.

frame

A **frame** is something that goes around a painting or a photograph. Mary's mother put the picture Mary painted at school in a **frame**.

free

If something is **free**, you don't have to pay any money to get it. The clown was giving away **free** balloons in the park.

freeze

When a liquid gets so cold it turns into ice, it **freezes**. In the winter the pond **freezes** and we go ice skating.

friend

A **friend** is someone you like to spend time with and who enjoys the same things you do. My **friend** and I like to play on the seesaw.

frog

A **frog** is a small animal that can live in or out of the water. A **frog** has long back legs for jumping and webbed feet to help it swim.

fruit

Fruit is food that grows on trees or bushes. Apples, bananas, and grapes are all **fruits** we like to eat.

full

Full means that something is holding as much as it can. The toy chest was so **full** the lid wouldn't close.

Gg

gather

To **gather** means to collect things or bring them together. The farmer **gathers** the eggs from the hen house and puts them in a basket every morning.

game

A **game** is an activity that is fun and amusing. Kevin wanted to play a board **game** indoors, but Amy wanted to go outside to play a **game** of tag.

gentle

Gentle means kind and mild. Uncle Ethan is a **gentle** person who has always taken care of animals.

garden

A **garden** is an area of ground where you can grow vegetables, fruits, or flowers. This year we added a row of lettuce to the **garden**.

globe

A **globe** is a map of the world that is shaped like a ball. There is a **globe** on the teacher's desk.

gate

A **gate** is an opening in a fence or a wall. The big iron **gate** into the park is open all day.

goat

A **goat** is a shaggy animal with hoofs, curved horns, and a short tail. **Goats** give milk which is good to drink or to make into cheese.

grandfather clock

A **grandfather clock** is a tall clock in a cabinet that stands on the floor. In the hallway of the old house there is a beautiful **grandfather clock**.

grow

To **grow** means to become bigger. Everything that is alive can **grow**. Jay hopes to **grow** as tall as his older brother.

grandparents

Your **grandparents** are the parents of your mother and the parents of your father. John loves to go visit his **grandparents** for summer vacation.

guess

If you **guess**, you may think something without knowing for sure if it is true. The girl tried to **guess** how many jelly beans were in the huge glass jar.

great

When something is **great**, it is bigger, better, or more special than usual. John's father gave him a **great** striped umbrella to use in the rain.

guinea pig

A **guinea pig** is a small, furry animal with short ears and a short tail. Lois has a **guinea pig** for a pet.

group

A **group** is a collection of people or things that belong together. A small **group** of children played together in the treehouse every afternoon.

guitar

A **guitar** is a musical instrument. It usually has six strings that are played with the fingers or with a small, flat pick. John plays the **guitar** in a band.

BIRDS

bluejay

stork

eagle

cardinal

hummingbird

speckled starling

robin

ostrich

rooster

sparrow

canary

quail

flamingo

pelican

parakeet

swan

duck

heron

falcon

hawk

turkey

dove

woodpecker

owl

blackbird

raven

pigeon

belted kingfisher

toucan

warbler

goldfinch

swallow

wren

parrot

gull

goose

spoonbill

penguin

pheasant

crane

vulture

puffin

condor

hangar

A **hangar** is a large building, like a garage, where airplanes are kept. The jumbo jet was taken to the **hangar** so the engine could be repaired.

half

A **half** of something is one of two equal parts that make up the whole. Annie gave **half** of her sandwich to her sister.

hard hat

A **hard hat** is a strong hat that construction workers wear to protect their heads. It was easy to spot the construction boss in his bright green **hard hat**.

hammer

A **hammer** is a tool that is used to pound nails into things. The carpenter used a **hammer** and nails to put the sign on the door.

headlights

Headlights are the special lights on the front of a car that show the road ahead. When it got dark, the driver turned on his **headlights** so he could see better.

hamster

A **hamster** is a small, mouselike animal with large pouches in its cheeks. The **hamster** at the pet store likes sunflower seeds.

healthy

When you are **healthy**, your body is strong and well. To stay **healthy**, you need to eat the right foods, get plenty of fresh air and exercise, and be sure to get enough sleep.

helicopter

A **helicopter** uses rotating blades, which are on top of it, to fly. A **helicopter** flies low in the sky for short distances.

help

When you **help** someone, you find a way to make something easier, faster, or nicer for that person. Sue **helps** her mother with the dishes.

hide

When you **hide** something, you put it someplace where other people can't see or find it. My little brother sometimes **hides** when it's time to go to bed.

hobby

A **hobby** is an activity you like to do because it is fun and interesting. Kay's **hobby** is photographing animals.

hope

If you **hope** for something, you wish that something you want very much will happen. I **hope** my parents will get me a puppy.

horse

A **horse** is a large animal that can pull a wagon or that people ride. A **horse** has four legs, hoofs, a mane, and a tail. The performer stood on the back of the prancing **horse**.

hospital

A **hospital** is a place that cares for people who are sick or hurt. Steve stayed overnight at the **hospital** when he broke his leg.

hurry

If you **hurry**, you move or do something very fast. Lisa had to **hurry** so she wouldn't miss the school bus.

imagination

When you use your **imagination**, you are able to think about something that isn't real. Frank used his **imagination** to see different animal shapes in the clouds.

I

I is the word you use when you talk or write about yourself. **I** am eight years old, and today **I** am having a birthday party.

important

If something is **important**, it matters very much. It is **important** that you give this note to the teacher, so you will be able to go on the class trip.

iceberg

An **iceberg** is a huge chunk of ice that floats in cold parts of the ocean. The captain spotted an **iceberg** just ahead of the ship.

in

In means that something is within a place. The kittens play **in** the box. **In** also means within a certain time. **In** the summer Fran likes to go swimming.

idea

An **idea** is a thought that is in your mind. Paul had a good **idea** for raising money to buy the teacher a gift.

include

To **include** means to have someone or something as part of a group. The children remembered to **include** the new girl in the class when they went out to play.

infant

An **infant** is a newborn baby. The father smiled as he held the **infant** in his arms.

invent

To **invent** means to make something no one has made before. Mike wanted to **invent** a robot that could make chocolate chip cookies.

ingredient

An **ingredient** is something that is part of a mixture. Carrots were an **ingredient** in the stew.

invite

When you **invite** someone, you ask that person to do something with you. Scott **invited** John to go on a picnic.

insect

An **insect** is a tiny animal with six legs. An **insect** may have wings. An ant, a bee, and a fly are all **insects**.

iron

An **iron** is a machine that is used to smooth the wrinkles out of cloth. Mother used the **iron** to press her dress.

instead

Instead means in place of. Tracy decided to put an orange **instead** of a plum in her lunch box.

island

An **island** is a body of land completely surrounded by water. The lighthouse is on a tiny **island** just off the coast.

jeep

A **jeep** is a partly open vehicle that can travel over rough ground. The campers needed a **jeep** to reach their mountain cabin.

jacket

A **jacket** is an item of clothing worn over the upper part of your body to keep you warm. Anne's new winter **jacket** has fur on the collar and cuffs.

jet airplane

A **jet airplane** is an airplane that flies very fast because it has powerful engines. A **jet airplane** can fly so fast it goes across the country in only a few hours.

jam

Jam is a food made of fruit cooked with sugar. Mother used blueberries to make **jam**.

jewelry

Jewelry is a colorful object that you wear to look pretty. Rings, earrings, bracelets, and necklaces are **jewelry**. The queen was wearing beautiful gold **jewelry**.

jar

A **jar** is a round glass container used to store food. Janet got out a **jar** of peanut butter and a **jar** of jelly to make a sandwich.

job

A **job** is work people do for money. Peter's father has a **job** as a train engineer.

34

jog

To **jog** means to run at a slow, steady pace. Daniel likes to **jog** around the track in the park.

join

When you **join** something, you become a member of a group. Meg wanted to **join** the chorus. When you **join** things, you put them together. The children **joined** hands to make a circle.

joke

A **joke** is something you say or do to make people laugh. As a **joke**, John put on a funny mask and pretended to be someone else when his mother answered the door.

journey

A **journey** is a long trip from one place to another place. Uncle David used a map to plan his **journey** across the country.

joy

Joy is a feeling of great happiness. Ann felt great **joy** when she opened the box and found the camera she had always wanted.

juggle

To **juggle** means to toss and catch several objects at the same time. The performer **juggled** three bowling pins while balancing a plate on top of a stick.

juicy

When food is **juicy**, it has a lot of liquid in it. The peaches made a **juicy** and delicious snack.

jungle

A **jungle** is a deep, dense forest found in hot, humid places. Monkeys swing from tall trees in the **jungle**.

Kk

key

A **key** is a small piece of metal that opens a lock. Jody found a **key** to open the old trunk in the attic.

kaleidoscope

A **kaleidoscope** is a tube containing bits of colored glass. When the end is held to the light and turned, the bits of glass change position and make beautiful patterns.

kick

To **kick** something means to hit it with your foot. John **kicked** the ball to his friend.

keep

If you **keep** something, you hold it or save it. Joey hoped his mother would let him **keep** the turtle he found in the backyard.

kind

Kind means gentle and nice. Ms. Rafferty is a **kind** person who likes to help others. **Kind** also means the group that something belongs to. A collie is a **kind** of dog.

kettle

A **kettle** is a pot used for boiling water. When the **kettle** starts whistling, the water will be hot enough to make tea.

king

A **king** is a man who rules a country. The **king** put on his crown and sat on his throne.

kiss

When you **kiss**, you touch a person with your lips to show that you care very much. Beth always **kisses** her brother goodnight before he goes to bed.

knit

To **knit** is to connect yarn with special needles to make clothes or blankets. Grandmother likes to **knit** socks for her grandchildren.

kitchen

A **kitchen** is a room in which food is cooked. Everyone waits in the **kitchen** while Dad makes his special pancakes.

knock

To **knock** means to hit something sharply with your knuckles to make a noise. Jim **knocked** on his brother's door to let him know it was time to wake up.

kite

A **kite** is a toy made of paper or cloth that flies at the end of a long string. Michelle has a purple and yellow **kite** that looks like a butterfly.

knot

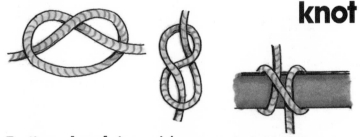

To tie a **knot**, two strings or ropes are twisted around each other and pulled tight. Sailors use many different kinds of **knots** on their boats.

kneel

When you **kneel**, you rest on your knees. The photographer had to **kneel** to take the girl's picture.

know

If you **know** something, you understand it or are sure of it. Do you **know** your address? If you **know** someone, you have met that person. Sue **knows** all the people on her street.

land

Land is the solid ground of the Earth. There are a lot of trees on our land. To land means to come down onto the ground. The seagull lands on the beach.

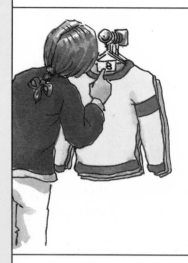

label

A label is something that identifies or describes an object. Mary looked at the label in the sweater to see if it was her size.

late

Late means to arrive or stay after the usual or proper time. Sam was late for school because he missed the bus.

ladder

A ladder is used to reach high places. It has two sides connected by rungs, which are like steps. Gus needed a ladder to paint the garage.

lawn mower

A lawn mower is a machine used to cut grass. Ann started to cut the grass, but the lawn mower ran out of gas before she could finish.

lamp

A lamp is a light. A lamp may be attached to a wall or ceiling, or it may be placed on a floor or a table. Jane turned on the lamp so she could read.

leaf

A leaf is the flat green part that grows on the branches of trees, plants, and bushes. In the spring and summer there are many leaves on the trees.

learn

If you **learn** something, you know about it by studying or practicing. Tina is **learning** how to play the piano.

lobster

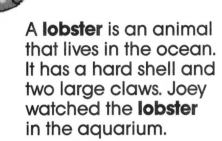

A **lobster** is an animal that lives in the ocean. It has a hard shell and two large claws. Joey watched the **lobster** in the aquarium.

library

A **library** is a place in which books and other reading material are kept. You can borrow books from the **library** to read at home. Peter read a magazine at the **library**.

logs

Logs are pieces of wood that are cut from a tree. **Logs** can be used as firewood or made into boards. The **logs** are stacked in the fireplace.

lifeguard

A **lifeguard** is an expert swimmer who watches out for the safety of other swimmers at a beach or pool. The **lifeguard** warned the children not to swim out too far.

long

When something is **long**, it means that one end of it is far away from the other end. A giraffe has a **long** neck.

lift

To **lift** something means to raise it up from a lower spot. A special truck at the airport **lifts** the cargo high enough to reach the airplane door.

love

To **love** someone means to care in a very special way for that person. Susie **loves** her grandfather very much.

IN THE HARBOR

Many boats pass through the harbor every day. Each one has a special job to do.

The huge **ocean liner** carries people across the sea. The **oil tanker**, the **container boat**, and the **freighter** carry every kind of cargo you can imagine—from food, to animals, to cars! These ships use powerful engines to make them go.

When the ships come into the harbor, a **tugboat** helps guide them safely to the **dock**. When the **freighter** is tied to its **mooring** workers begin unloading the cargo. A special **loading crane** lifts the huge **shipping crates** off the ship onto a **freight truck**.

Boats like the **clipper ship**, the **sloop**, and the **sailboat** use a system of **masts** and **sails** to make them go. The wind fills the sails, which pushes the boat through the water. A long time ago, before there were **ocean liners** and freighters, **clipper ships** were used to carry people and cargo across the ocean.

The powerful engines of the **hovercraft** raise it up and it glides across the water on a cushion of air. Both the **hovercraft** and the **ferry** carry people and cargo short distances.

Small boats, like the **canoe**, the **rowboat**, and the **raft**, need a person with **paddles** or **oars** to make them go.

All the boats depend on the **lighthouse**. It's strong beam of light guides them safely into and out of the **harbor**.

lighthouse

container boat

smokestacks

lifeboats

bridge

ocean liner

ferry

bell buoy

hovercraft

speedboat

tugboat

barge

motorboat

mast

outboard motor

sport-fishing boat

sloop

sailboat

cabin

buoy

rudder

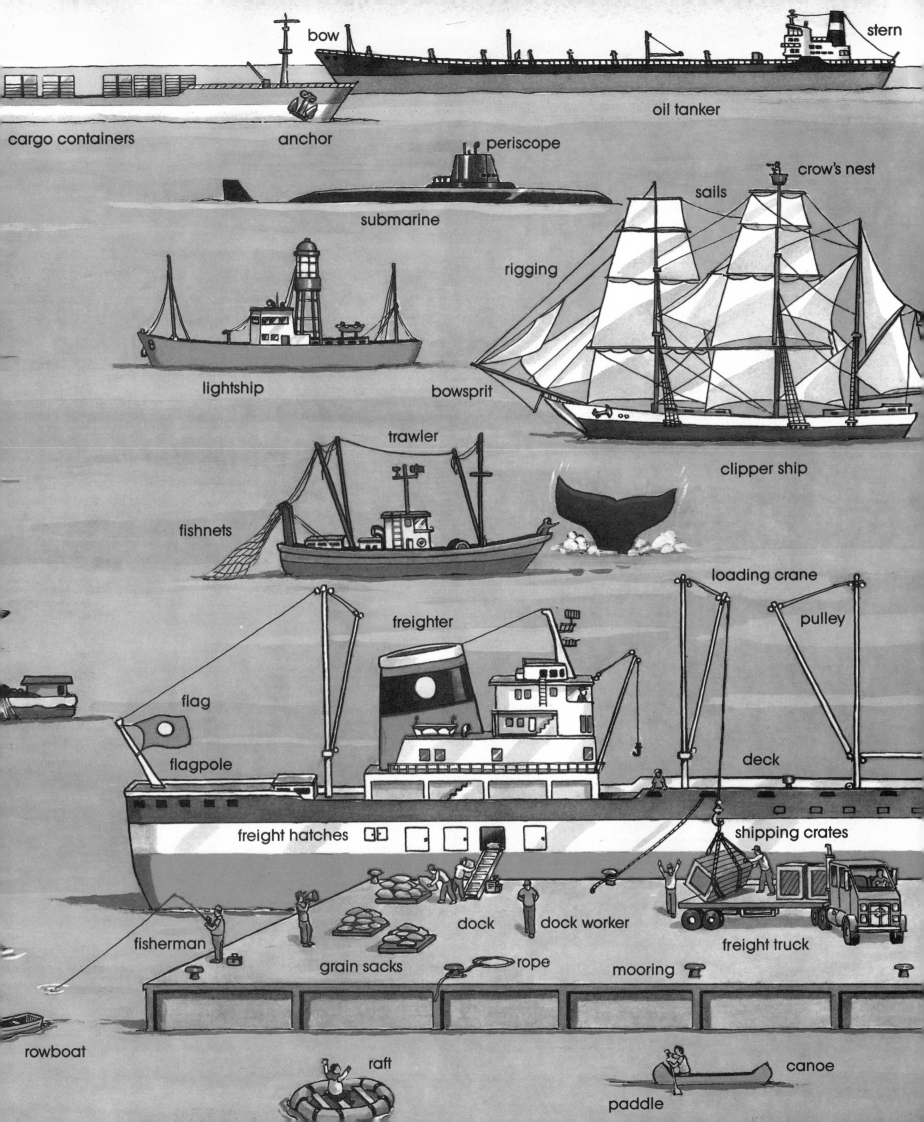

bow

stern

oil tanker

cargo containers

anchor

periscope

crow's nest

sails

submarine

rigging

lightship

bowsprit

clipper ship

trawler

fishnets

loading crane

pulley

freighter

flag

flagpole

deck

freight hatches

shipping crates

fisherman

dock

dock worker

freight truck

grain sacks

rope

mooring

rowboat

raft

canoe

paddle

Mm

match

When things **match**, they are alike or they belong together. The two striped socks **match**, but the polka-dot one doesn't.

magazine

A **magazine** is a collection of stories or articles that is published regularly. Beth read a **magazine** about sports.

measure

If you **measure** something, you find out how much it weighs, how tall or long it is, or how much space it fills. Peter **measured** his dog with a yardstick.

magic

Magic is the ability to make impossible things seem real. The clown at the circus did **magic** tricks and pulled a rabbit out of a hat.

medicine

Medicine is a pill or a liquid that helps you get better when you are sick. Only a doctor or your parents should give you **medicine**. Ed's mother gave him a spoonful of **medicine**.

map

A **map** is a drawing of a place. A **map** may show countries, roads, or the shape of the land. A huge **map** of the world hung at the front of the classroom.

microscope

A **microscope** is used to make very tiny things look large. With a **microscope** you can see things that are too small for your eyes alone to see.

middle

The **middle** is the center of something. It is an equal distance from the beginning and the end. In the photograph Wendy is in the **middle**, between her parents.

mix

When you **mix** things, you stir them together. Lori **mixed** blue and yellow paint together to make green paint.

minute

A **minute** is a short amount of time. There are 60 seconds in one **minute**, and 60 **minutes** in one hour. It takes Paul about a **minute** to tie his shoes.

mobile

A **mobile** is an ornament made by hanging objects from string or wire so they move in a breeze. Patty made a **mobile** of yellow paper birds and hung it over the baby's crib.

mirror

A **mirror** is a special glass in which you can see yourself. When you comb your hair, it helps to look in a **mirror** so you can see what you're doing.

money

Money is what you use to buy things. Dollars, dimes, and nickels are **money**. Susie saved enough **money** to buy some new roller skates.

mistake

A **mistake** is something that is incorrect. Simon made a **mistake** on his math homework. Can you find it?

monkey

A **monkey** is a furry animal with a long tail. **Monkeys** use their feet like hands to help them climb trees and swing from branches.

motorcycle

A **motorcycle** is a vehicle that looks like a big bicycle with an engine. The bright purple **motorcycle** is parked in the yard.

muscle

Muscle is the soft part of your body that helps you move. **Muscles** can stretch out and pull back. If you bend your arm you can feel the **muscle**.

mountain

A **mountain** is a rocky area of land that rises high above the earth around it. The **mountain** was so high it had snow on the top.

music

Music is a mixture of sounds that is pleasant to hear. People sing or play instruments to make **music**. Bill likes to listen to **music** on the radio.

mouse

A **mouse** is a small, furry animal with round ears, a pointed nose, and a long tail. A cat chased the **mouse** around the barn.

must

If you **must** do something, you have to do it. You **must** put a stamp on the letter before you mail it.

move

To **move** means to go or carry something from one place to another. Michael **moved** his books from the floor to the table.

mystery

A **mystery** is something that you don't understand or can't explain. It is a **mystery** how the kitten got to the top of the cabinet.

Nn

need

If you **need** something, you must have it. You **need** boots and mittens to play outside in the snow.

name

A **name** is a word that tells who or what something is. A person has a first **name**, sometimes a middle **name**, and a last **name**. Mary put her **name** at the top of her painting.

neighbor

A **neighbor** is a person who lives near you. Mrs. Brown talked to her next-door **neighbor**.

nature

Nature is all of the living world that is not made by people. Plants and animals are part of **nature**. When you are out in the woods **nature** is all around you.

nest

A **nest** is a home made out of sticks or dry grass by a bird or other animal. There are three eggs in the bird's **nest** in the apple tree.

near

Near means close to or a short distance from someone or something. The puppies played **near** their mother.

net

A **net** is used to catch things. It can be made of string, rope, or wire. Nicholas used a **net** to catch a butterfly, which he later let go.

newspaper

A **newspaper** tells people what is happening in their town or in the world. My father reads the **newspaper** every evening.

nothing

Nothing means not one thing. Someone had eaten all the cookies, and there was **nothing** in the jar.

nibble

When you **nibble** something, you take tiny bites of it. The rabbit **nibbled** on the carrot.

notice

If you **notice** something, you look at it or become aware of it. Julie **noticed** that Ken was wearing one green sock and one yellow sock.

noisy

Noisy means making a loud sound. The jackhammer was so **noisy** that the man covered his ears.

noun

A **noun** is the name of a person, place, or thing. Bill wrote a list of **nouns** on the blackboard.

noon

Noon is 12 o'clock, the middle of the day. The children eat lunch every day at **noon**.

nurse

A **nurse** is a person who takes care of you when you are in the hospital. The **nurse** gave Joey his medicine.

octopus

An **octopus** is an ocean animal that has eight arms called *tentacles*. The **octopus** held onto the rocks with its tentacles.

obey

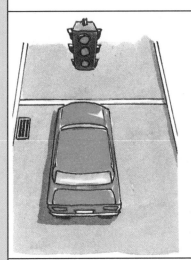

If you **obey**, you follow rules or behave as you are told. The driver of the car **obeyed** the traffic light.

odor

An **odor** is a smell. When it is frightened, a skunk gives off a strong **odor**.

ocean

An **ocean** is a body of salt water that covers a large part of the earth. Ann loves to go to the **ocean** and swim in the waves.

office

An **office** is a place where people work. Gina spent the afternoon at her mother's **office**.

octagon

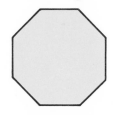

An **octagon** is a shape with eight sides. The sign over the door of the restaurant was shaped like an **octagon**.

old

Old means not new. It is best to wear **old** clothes when you paint. If someone is **old** it means they have lived a long time. My grandmother is **old**.

open

If something is **open** it means you can get in or out of it. The door to the basement is **open**.

oval

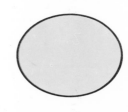

An **oval** is a shape that resembles an egg. An olive is shaped like an **oval**.

opposite

When things are **opposite**, they are as different as they can be. Day is the **opposite** of night. Big is the **opposite** of little.

overflow

To **overflow** means to pour over the top. Someone forgot to turn off the faucet and the water **overflowed**.

organize

When you **organize** something, you arrange it in a way that is neat or easy to find. Mother **organized** the silverware so it would be easy to find the spoons and forks.

owl

An **owl** is a bird with a large head, round eyes, and a hooked beak. **Owls** sleep in the day and hunt for food at night. The **owl** made its nest in a hole in the tree.

our

Our means belonging to us. **Our** house is the only white and green one on the street.

own

If you **own** something, it belongs to you. Janet **owns** a red sweater with her name on it.

Pp

park

A **park** is an area with trees, flowers, grass, and sometimes fountains, that is for everyone to enjoy. There is a new playground at the **park**.

pair

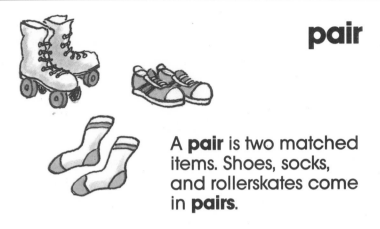

A **pair** is two matched items. Shoes, socks, and rollerskates come in **pairs**.

pass

Pass means to hand something to someone. Please **pass** the salt. Also, if you **pass** something, you go by it. Cheryl and Dick **pass** the library on their way to school.

parade

A **parade** is a group of people who march together to celebrate a special event. Our town has a **parade** every year at the beginning of spring.

path

A **path** is a trail that you can follow. There is a bike **path** around the lake.

parents

Your **parents** are your mother and father. Lori's **parents** took her to the zoo.

patient

A **patient** is a person who is receiving care in a hospital. Noah is a **patient** at the hospital. To be **patient** means that you can wait quietly for something.

peek

If you **peek** at something, you take a quick look at it. Sam **peeked** into the box.

pilot

A **pilot** is a person who controls an aircraft, a spacecraft, or a ship. The **pilot** checked with the control tower before taking off.

permission

If you ask **permission** to do something, you ask if you are allowed to do it. Kathy asked for **permission** to use the scissors.

pipe

A **pipe** is a long, hollow tube through which liquid or gas can travel. The huge **pipes** that carry water are laid in the ground piece by piece.

pet

A **pet** is an animal that lives with you and that you take care of. Marty has a dog and two cats as **pets**.

pitchfork

A **pitchfork** is a tool with sharp prongs used for picking up and moving hay. The farmer used a **pitchfork** to get hay down from the loft.

piano

A **piano** is a large musical instrument. It has 88 keys that make music when they are pressed. Susie practiced a song on the **piano**.

plan

When you **plan** something, you think about it before you do it. A **plan** is also an idea or instructions explaining how to do something. The builder studied the **plans** for the new house.

plants

Plants are all living things that are not animals. **Plants** need light and water to grow. Mary put her **plants** near the window to give them some light.

plenty

Plenty means there is enough of something. There was **plenty** of cake for everyone at the picnic.

pocket

A **pocket** is sewn into or onto your clothes so that you can carry things. Jane had her keys and a comb in her **pocket**.

point

When you **point**, you use your finger to show where something is. The teacher **pointed** to the blackboard. A **point** is also the sharp end of something. Jane stuck the **point** of the pin into the pincushion.

polite

To be **polite** means to use good manners and be nice to other people. John was **polite** and held the door open for his mother.

portrait

A **portrait** is a painting, a photograph, or a drawing of a person. Many **portraits** hang in the museum.

pots

A **pot** is a metal container with handles used for cooking. Mom made soup in a big **pot**.

pour

Pour means to move liquid from one place to another. The water **poured** out of the faucet.

practice

When you **practice** something, you do it again and again so that you can do it better. Linda **practiced** the song on her violin for more than an hour.

promise

If you **promise**, you say that you really will do something. The children **promised** not to touch the cake until the party.

present

A **present** is something you give to someone for a special reason. Robert wrapped the **present** for his sister and tied it with a big red bow.

proud

When you feel **proud**, you feel glad that you have done something very well. Sue was **proud** of the picture she painted in school.

price

The **price** is how much something costs. The **price** of a carton of milk is twenty-five cents.

pull

If you **pull** something, you move it toward you. The farmer used a tractor to **pull** the bales of hay.

prize

A **prize** is something given to you for winning a contest or doing something very well. The swimmer who won the race received a trophy as a **prize**.

puzzle

A **puzzle** is a problem or a game that you try to put together or figure out. Rachel is trying to put the **puzzle** together.

quick

If something is **quick**, it is fast. The rabbit was so **quick** the dog couldn't catch it.

quarter

A **quarter** is one of four equal pieces that together make a whole. Each **quarter** of the circle is a different color.

quiet

If something is **quiet**, it doesn't make any noise. Billy was **quiet** while his mother read him a story.

queen

A **queen** is a woman who rules a country. The **queen** wore a long cape and a crown for the ceremony.

quilt

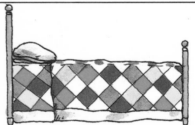

A **quilt** is a special blanket that is stuffed with soft material and covered by cloth sewn in a special design. At the inn, the bed was covered by a beautiful patchwork **quilt**.

question

A **question** is what you ask when you want to know something. Lisa asked the teacher a **question** about the homework, and the teacher gave her an answer.

quit

To **quit** means to stop doing something. Billy **quit** picking apples when he filled the basket.

SEA ANIMALS

swordfish

humpback whale

flippers

killer whale

diver

harpoon

squid

anchor

shark

jellyfish

stingray

seaweed

octopus

radiator

A **radiator** is a metal object that gives off heat to warm a room. The **radiator** made a soft, hissing sound as it warmed up.

rabbit

A **rabbit** is a soft, furry animal with long ears, a fluffy tail, and strong back legs for hopping. The **rabbit** hopped into the garden to eat the lettuce.

raft

A **raft** is a small wooden or rubber boat. The children paddled across the pond on the **raft**.

raccoon

A **raccoon** is a furry animal with dark patches around its eyes and dark rings around its tail. The **raccoon** rinsed its food off in the stream.

raincoat

A **raincoat** is a jacket or coat made of material that keeps you from getting wet in the rain. Robbie has a new yellow **raincoat**.

race

When you **race**, you try to move faster than another person. Two members of the ski team **raced** down the mountain.

reach

To **reach** means to stretch out to get something. Sharon had to **reach** to get her scarf down from the closet shelf.

ready

When you are **ready**, you are prepared to do something. Once Betsy had on her mask, inner tube, and flippers, she was **ready** to go swimming.

remember

When you **remember** something, you think of it again. When Susan looked at the photograph it helped her **remember** her party.

real

Real means true, not make-believe. Wayne wasn't sure if the mouse was made of rubber, or if it was **real**.

repeat

If you **repeat** something, you say or do it again. Andy wrote his name on the blackboard and then **repeated** it.

record

A **record** is a circle of plastic with special grooves that makes music when you put it on a record player. Sally played the **record** of her favorite song.

restaurant

A **restaurant** is a place where you pay to have someone cook and serve you a meal. This **restaurant** offers many different kinds of food.

refrigerator

A **refrigerator** is a household machine that keeps food cold and fresh. We keep fruits, vegetables, milk, and eggs in the **refrigerator**.

return

To **return** means to give back or to go back. Wanda's new sweater was too big, so she **returned** it to the store.

right

Right is the direction that is the opposite of left. Raise your **right** hand if you have a question. If something is **right**, it is correct. Patty gave all the **right** answers on the test.

robot

A **robot** is a machine that can follow directions to do some of the same work that people do. The toy **robot** moved forward and backward on command.

rocking chair

A **rocking chair** is a chair with a curved bottom that rocks back and forth. It is fun to sit in grandfather's old **rocking chair**.

roof

The **roof** is the top covering of a building. We had our **roof** fixed because it was leaking.

rough

Rough means bumpy and uneven. The bark of the tree feels **rough**.

row

A **row** is a line of things. Audrey sat in the front **row** of the theater. To **row** also means to move a boat by using oars. We like to **row** our boat across the lake.

runway

A **runway** is a strip of paved, open ground on which an airplane takes off and lands. The jet was just about to touch down on the **runway**.

rush

If you **rush**, you do something fast or in a short time. Tim **rushed** to grab the vase before it fell.

Ss

saw

A **saw** is a tool used for cutting a hard object such as wood or metal. Dad used a **saw** to cut down the tree.

sad

If you are **sad**, it means you are not happy about something. Ann was **sad** when her dog hurt its paw.

scaffold

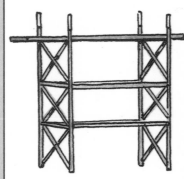

A **scaffold** is a platform used by workers high above the ground. The painters used a **scaffold** to reach the second floor of the house.

safe

When you are **safe**, you are not in any danger. We were **safe** from the storm inside the house.

scale

A **scale** is a machine that measures the weight of people or things. The nurse weighed Anne on the **scale** when she was at the doctor's office.

save

If you **save** something, you keep it. Peggy likes to **save** her money in a piggybank.

scuba diver

A **scuba diver** is a person who can swim underwater using special equipment. The **scuba diver** put on his wetsuit, mask, fins, and tanks of air before he went into the water.

sea horse

A **sea horse** is a small ocean animal with a head and neck that make it look a little bit like a horse. Carmen watched the **sea horse** swim around the aquarium.

senses

Your **senses** tell you about the world around you. You have five **senses**—sight, hearing, taste, smell, and touch. Your **sense** of smell doesn't work very well when you have a cold.

seal

A **seal** is an animal that lives alongside the ocean. A **seal** has smooth fur and webbed flippers which it uses for swimming. The **seal** dove in the water to catch a fish.

sewing machine

A **sewing machine** is a machine that stitches cloth together with thread. You can save time patching pants if you use a **sewing machine**.

search

When you **search** for something, you look for it. Aunt Mary **searched** for her lost earring.

share

When you **share**, you give some part of what you have to someone else. Ellen **shared** her orange with her friend.

season

A **season** is a part of the year. There are four **seasons** in a year—spring, summer, autumn, and winter. Spring is Scott's favorite **season** because he likes to work in the garden.

shed

A **shed** is a small building used for storing tools and other items outdoors. The rake is in the **shed**.

sheep

A **sheep** is an animal whose woolly coat is used to make yarn and cloth. The farmer has 25 **sheep** on his farm.

shopping cart

A **shopping cart** is a metal basket on wheels that you use in a store to carry the things you are buying. At the grocery store, the **shopping carts** are near the entrance.

shovel

A **shovel** is a tool with a wide piece of metal and a long handle that you use for digging and lifting. Use a **shovel** to turn over the dirt in the garden.

show

When you **show** something, you let someone else see it. Ellen **showed** her brother the worm she found in the garden.

skateboard

A **skateboard** is a narrow board on wheels that you stand on and ride. Jason wore a helmet and kneepads when he rode his **skateboard**.

skeleton

A **skeleton** is the framework of bones that holds up a body. A **skeleton** hangs in the science lab.

skis

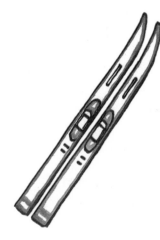

Skis are long pieces of wood, metal, or plastic that are used to glide over snow or water. Mary couldn't wait for the first snow so she could try her new **skis**.

skunk

A **skunk** is an animal with black and white fur that gives off a strong, unpleasant odor when it is frightened. Ron saw a **skunk** run across his backyard.

sled

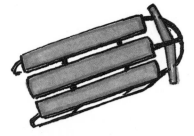

A **sled** is a wooden platform on runners that travels over snow. Amy went down the big hill in the park on her **sled**.

soak

If you **soak** something, you put it in water until it is thoroughly wet. Mother **soaked** her tired feet in warm water.

slice

To **slice** something means to cut it with a knife. Dad **sliced** a piece of cheese for Ruth's sandwich. A **slice** is a thin piece cut from a large piece. Ruth put the cheese between two **slices** of bread.

spell

When you **spell**, you put letters together to make a word. Susie's mother taught her how to **spell** her name.

slippers

Slippers are a kind of soft, comfortable shoe that you wear indoors. Woody has a new pair of blue **slippers**.

spider

A **spider** is a bug that has eight legs and can spin a web. The **spider** made a big web in the garden.

snake

A **snake** is a reptile with scales and a long narrow body. It has no legs. The **snake** slithered through the grass.

square

A **square** is a shape that has four equal sides. The picture and the window are **squares**.

squirrel

A **squirrel** is a small animal with a bushy tail that usually lives in trees. The **squirrel** was eating an acorn.

station wagon

A **station wagon** is a kind of car with an extra set of seats and a rear door that opens. There are so many people in John's family they need a **station wagon**.

steamroller

A **steamroller** is a machine with huge, wide rollers that smooths down roads. After the asphalt was laid on the new road, the **steamroller** smoothed it out.

still

To be **still** means to not move or make any noise. When Tim saw the deer he stood very **still** so as not to frighten it. If something is **still** happening, it means that it is continuing to happen.

streetlight

A **streetlight** is a light on top of a tall pole that lights the streets and roads at night. The **streetlight** helps drivers see at night.

sweep

To **sweep** means to clean a surface using a broom or brush. The clerk at the grocery store **swept** the floor.

swimming pool

A **swimming pool** is a place where one swims. It is usually made of concrete and filled with water. We like to go to the **swimming pool** in the summer.

swing set

A **swing set** is a large outdoor toy with swings and rings, and sometimes a ladder or slide. I like to play on my **swing set**.

team

A **team** is a group of people that does something together. The **team** that John plays with has blue and white uniforms.

take

If you **take** something, you put it into your own hands. **Take** also means to carry. The boys **take** their lunches to school every day.

telephone

A **telephone** is a machine that lets you talk to someone in another place. Joan can talk on the **telephone** to her aunt who lives in another town.

tall

If something is **tall**, it is higher than most other things around it. The giraffe is the **tallest** animal in the zoo.

telescope

A **telescope** is an instrument used to look at objects in the sky that are very far away. The stars looked very bright and close through the **telescope**.

teach

To **teach** means to show someone how to do something or help them to understand something. Kelly tried to **teach** her younger sister how to tie her shoes.

tent

A **tent** is an outdoor shelter made of canvas. It is held up by poles and ropes. The campers set up their **tent** near the lake.

thank

When you **thank** people, you say how much you like what they gave you or did for you. Todd wrote a letter to **thank** his cousins for the book on dinosaurs.

tie

When you **tie** something, you fasten it together with a knot. Father **tied** the package with string before he mailed it.

theater

A **theater** is a place where movies are shown or plays are performed. A new adventure movie opened at the **theater** this week.

tile

A **tile** is a smooth, hard, colorful square made of stone, clay or some other material that is used to decorate walls or floors. The **tile** in the bathroom is pink and yellow.

think

When you **think**, you use your mind to create an idea. The teacher told us to **think** carefully before we wrote down our answers.

time

Time is the way we measure when something happens or how long it takes for it to happen. At three o'clock it is **time** to go home from school.

throw

If you **throw** something, you send it through the air. Pete **throws** sticks for his dog to catch.

toaster

A **toaster** is a household machine that makes bread warm and crunchy. Dennis put two slices of bread in the **toaster** for breakfast.

toboggan

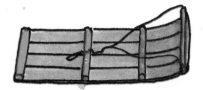

A **toboggan** is a long wooden sled with a flat bottom and a curved front that rides on snow. Alicia rode down the steep hill on her **toboggan**.

together

Together means all in one place or as a group. The children played **together** in the sandbox.

toss

If you **toss** something, you throw it lightly into the air. The boys play a game where they try to **toss** a ring onto a stick.

town

A **town** is a place where people live and work. A **town** is smaller than a city. Our **town** has a post office, a fire station, a library, and some stores.

trade

When you **trade**, you give someone something and that person gives you something in return. Mary **traded** her book on dinosaurs for one of John's fish.

train

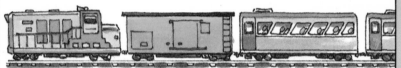

A **train** is a line of railroad cars drawn by an engine over tracks that cover long distances. **Trains** carry people and cargo across the country.

travel

When you **travel**, you go from one place to another. We **travel** to the beach many times during the summer.

tree

A **tree** is a large plant with one main woody trunk and many branches. Some **trees** have needles that stay green all year. Other **trees** have leaves that change color in the autumn.

triangle

A **triangle** is a shape with three straight sides and three corners. Some flags and boat sails are shaped like **triangles**.

trick

A **trick** is something done to fool someone. For his first **trick**, the magician pulled a string of scarves from his pocket.

tricycle

A **tricycle** is a vehicle that small children ride. It has three wheels, handlebars, a seat, and pedals. Neil rode his **tricycle** around the driveway.

trust

When you **trust** people, you believe in what they say and do. My parents **trust** me to take good care of my new kitten.

try

When you **try** to do something, you attempt to do it. Joan **tried** to reach the light switch but it was too high. **Try** also means to test or taste. Martin **tried** the fish and liked it.

turn

To **turn** means to move around. Mother **turned** the steering wheel to make the car go left. A **turn** is also a chance to do something. It's Charlie's **turn** to use the swing.

turtle

A **turtle** is an animal with short legs and a hard shell that protects its body. **Turtles** can live on land and in the water.

typewriter

A **typewriter** is a machine that prints letters when you press keys on a board. Ross practices on the **typewriter** in his parents' office.

Uu

under

Under means below or beneath something. Martha found her missing sneaker **under** the bed.

ugly

If something is **ugly** it is unpleasant to look at. Cathy drew a picture of an **ugly** monster.

understand

When you **understand** something, you know it or have a clear idea about it. Casey and his brother **understand** the rules for playing chess.

umbrella

An **umbrella** is a shade made of cloth that opens and closes to protect you from rain or sun. A white and yellow **umbrella** covers the table on the porch.

unicorn

A **unicorn** is an imaginary animal that looks like a horse with a long horn in the middle of its forehead. There are many fairytales written about **unicorns**.

uncle

Your **uncle** is the brother of your mother or father. Your **uncle** is also the husband of your aunt. **Uncle** Henry and Aunt Alice came to visit.

uniform

A **uniform** is a special outfit worn by people who belong to a group of some kind. The airline pilots all wore blue **uniforms**.

unique

If something is **unique**, it is special and there is nothing else like it. Since Henry's mother knit a one-of-a-kind sweater, it was **unique**.

upstairs

Upstairs means on an upper floor of a building. All the bedrooms in our house are **upstairs**.

untie

To **untie** means to take out a knot and loosen the ropes or laces that fasten something. Jimmy **untied** the dog's rope so she could run around the yard.

us

Us means you and me and other people. Dad took **us** to the store with him.

upset

To **upset** someone means to make them worried or angry. **Upset** also means to knock over. When Sam reached for the salt he **upset** the glass of juice.

use

Use means to do something with the help of another object. Mother taught the baby to **use** a spoon instead of her fingers to eat her food.

upside-down

Upside-down means the top is on the bottom, and the bottom is on the top. John likes to stand on his head and look at everything **upside-down**.

usually

Usually means done in the normal way or done very often. Sandy **usually** stops for her friend Ann on the way to school.

ON THE RAILROAD

The **train station** is a very busy place. Many different kinds of trains come and go all day long.

The **stationmaster** makes sure everything runs smoothly and that the trains are on time.

The **freight train** is made up of many types of cars which carry everything from coal in a **hopper** to gasoline in a **tank car**. Animals are often carried in the **cattle car**. There is even a **refrigerator car** to carry cargo that must be kept cold.

The **steam locomotive** was used many years ago to carry people and cargo across the country. The engine was fueled with coal that was carried in a special **coal car** behind it. The **cowcatcher** on the front helped keep the tracks clear. When the train traveled at night the only light came from the **headlamp**.

Many modern trains are powered by electricity. The **electric locomotive** uses electricity supplied by **electric lines**. A **high-speed engine** often uses electricity as well. This engine usually pulls **passenger cars** and can take travelers from one place to another very quickly.

Another type of train that uses electricity is the **monorail**, which carries its **passengers** on a special overhead track in the air!

The **diesel switcher** at the station makes sure that all these trains arrive and depart on the right tracks.

It looks like the **porter** is getting ready to load the baggage. All aboard!

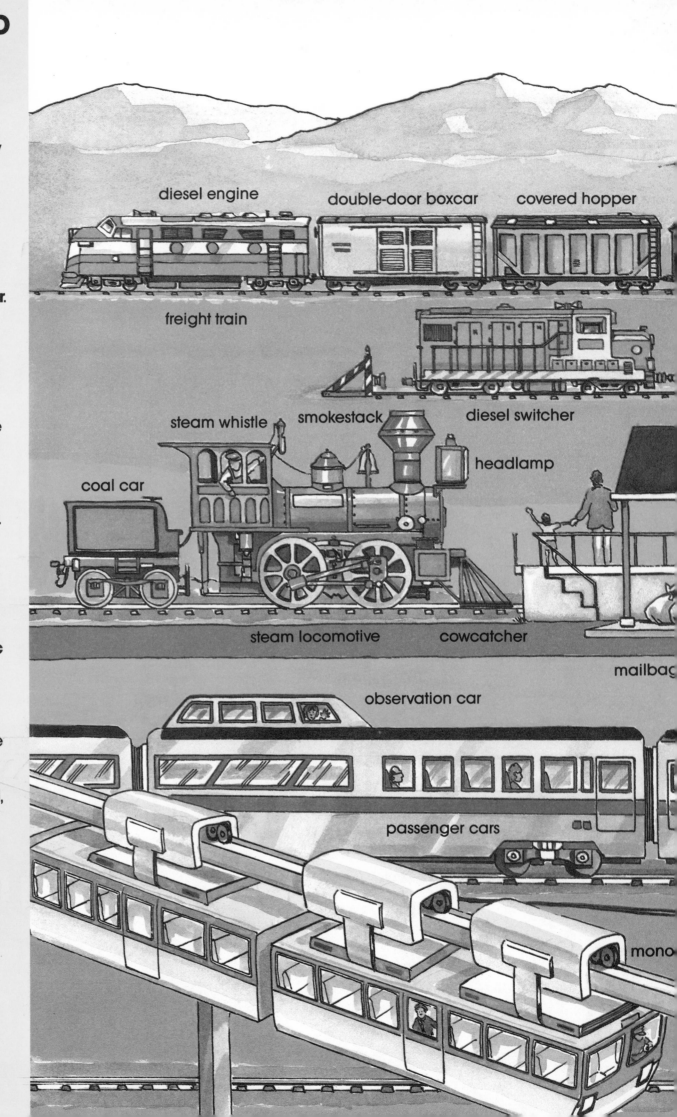

diesel engine

double-door boxcar

covered hopper

freight train

steam whistle

smokestack

diesel switcher

headlamp

coal car

steam locomotive

cowcatcher

mailbag

observation car

passenger cars

mono

cog railway

tunnel

hopper

refrigerator car

piggyback car

cattle car

tank car

flatcar

gondola car

ane car

super flatcar

station

signal light

platform

lantern

brakeman

passenger

stationmaster

caboose

porter

ticket window

dining car

high-speed engine

horn

bumper

engineer

electric lines

headlights

electric locomotive

Vv

vase

A **vase** is a container for flowers. Susan put a beautiful bouquet of wildflowers in a red **vase**.

valley

A **valley** is a low area of land that lies between two mountains. A herd of cows was grazing in the **valley**.

vegetable

A **vegetable** is a plant that can be eaten. Foods such as beans, carrots, potatoes, and squash are **vegetables**. There are many kinds of **vegetables** for sale at the farm.

valuable

Something that is **valuable** is worth a lot of money or is very important. The painting was very **valuable** because it could not be replaced.

vending machine

A **vending machine** is a machine that gives out an item when you put in the right amount of money. You can buy soda, candy, or fruit from a **vending machine**.

van

A **van** is a large box-like car that has extra room to carry passengers or to deliver things from stores. The flowers for mother came from the florist in a **van**.

very

Very means more than usual. The soup had been on the stove for a long time so it was **very** hot when James started to eat it.

veterinarian

A **veterinarian** is a doctor who takes care of animals. The **veterinarian** bandaged the dog's hurt paw.

visit

When you **visit**, you go to see a person or a place. Aunt Helen came to **visit** mother this afternoon.

view

A **view** is a scene that you see. We had a nice **view** of the harbor from the balcony.

voice

Your **voice** is the sound that comes out of your mouth when you talk. My dog recognizes the sound of my **voice** when I call him.

vine

A **vine** is a plant with a long stem that runs along the ground or up a wall. The **vines** grew up the front of the cottage.

volcano

A **volcano** is a mountain that sometimes pours out very hot, melted rocks from the center of the earth. When the **volcano** erupted lava poured down the mountain.

violin

A **violin** is a musical instrument with four strings. You play the **violin** by drawing a bow across it. Sam played the **violin** at the recital.

vote

When you **vote**, you say whether you want or do not want something. Everyone who **voted** for the team to wear red t-shirts raised their hands.

Ww

weak

Weak means not strong or powerful. Bobby was too **weak** to lift the heavy box.

waiter

A **waiter** is a person who serves you your meal in a restaurant. The **waiter** put a basket of bread in the middle of the table.

weasel

A **weasel** is a small slender animal that lives in the woods. We saw a **weasel** on our camping trip.

want

When you **want** something, you would like to have it or to take part in an activity. The dog **wants** to go for a walk.

week

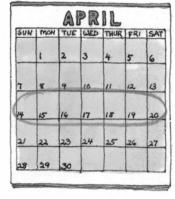

A **week** is seven days. The days of the **week** are Sunday, Monday, Tuesday, Wednesday, Thursday, Friday, and Saturday. Karen drew a line on the calendar around the **week** she was going on vacation.

wave

When you **wave**, you use your hand to say hello or goodbye to someone. Amanda **waved** to her friend in the park. A **wave** is also water in the ocean that rises up and then down.

weld

To **weld** means to join two pieces of metal by melting them together. In the factory, a worker had to **weld** the corners of the red wagon.

whale

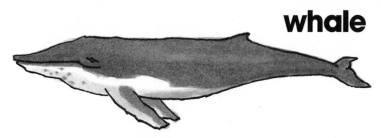

A **whale** is a very large ocean animal with front flippers, a flat tail, and a nose at the top of its body. The **whale** swam deep in the ocean.

win

When you **win**, you do something faster or better than everyone else. Jill's turtle was way ahead of the other turtles and was going to **win** the race.

when

When is a word used to ask a question or make a statement about time. Danny wanted to know **when** dinner would be ready.

window

A **window** is an opening in a wall that lets in light or air. Andy closed the **window** when it started to rain.

where

Where is a word used to ask or tell about the location of a place. Frank asked **where** he should put the clean dishes.

wish

If you **wish**, you hope for something that seems impossible to happen. Dana **wished** for a new bike when she blew out the candles on the cake.

whisper

If you **whisper**, you speak in a very soft, low voice so that you cannot be heard by everyone. Jacqueline **whispered** to her friend Kim so she wouldn't disturb anyone.

wonderful

If something is **wonderful**, it is especially good. The children had a **wonderful** time at the beach.

75

Xx

x-ray

An **x-ray** is a picture that is taken by a special machine of the inside of something. A doctor takes an **x-ray** of a part of your body to see if anything is wrong.

xylophone

A **xylophone** is a musical instrument that has metal bars that you hit with wooden hammers. Sally played a tune on the **xylophone** for her brother.

Yy

yawn

When you **yawn**, you open your mouth wide and take a deep breath. You **yawn** when you are tired.

yell

If you **yell**, you say something in a very loud voice. Father **yelled** out the back door that it was time for dinner.

yes

When you say **yes**, you agree with someone or you agree to do something. Mother said **yes** when we asked if we could go fishing.

Zz

A **zinnia** is a small plant with colorful, long-lasting flowers. The garden path was lined with **zinnias**.

zebra

A **zebra** is a black-and-white striped animal that looks like a horse and lives in Africa. The **zebra** galloped across the open plain.

zone

A **zone** is an area clearly marked for a special reason. Mike couldn't park in front of the hotel because it was a no-parking **zone**.

zero

Two minus two is **zero**. It is written **0** and means none. Two minus two is **zero**.

zoo

A **zoo** is a place where animals are kept so that people can see them. I like to look at the monkeys when we go to the **zoo**.

zigzag

A **zigzag** is a pattern of straight lines that makes short, sharp turns. The road made a **zigzag** up the side of the mountain.

Aa

awning

Bb

barn

Cc

cement mixer

Gg

globe

Hh

helicopter

Ii

island

Mm
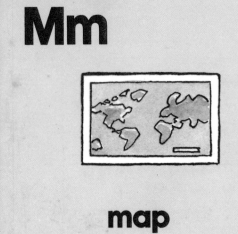
map

Nn

net

Oo

octopus

Ss

sled

Tt

tree

Uu

umbrella